The Becoming

Pashance A.

Metamorphosis Diaries

Book I

Copyright © 2023 by **Pashance A.**

All rights reserved. This book or any portion thereof may not be reproduced or used in any manner whatsoever without the express written permission of the publisher except for the use of brief quotations in a book review.

Table of Contents

I. The Cocoon
A Lonely New Years Eve   1

II. Operation Rehab
Face Me Sober   11

III. Uprooting This House
Mirror My Mirror   29

IV. Bloom
Like A Lotus   35

V. Good Morning
The Unfinished Work   39

VI. Baptized In Light
Transformation Butterfly   45

Oftentimes our deepest fears derive from the truths' that we haven't allowed ourselves to face.

The silence of this room amplifies the chaos in the mind.

Are you brave enough to play the quiet game with me anyway?

When it's all over, we both will have won.

I'll go first…

I

The Cocoon

A LONELY NEW YEARS EVE

I Am beginning to wonder how long I have been on autopilot. Frankly, the taunting of my past changes as I mature into my womanhood. However, the shadows of my life before, still haunt me today. I have gone through most of my life as a bystander to my own reality. Hardly recognizing the girl, to the young woman, I have camouflaged into. My life at seventeen is still a vivid memory of yesterday, yet four years have passed since then. What is to become of me now?

As 2022 begins, the clock strikes 12:31 AM, and my heart feels unbearably heavy. For the longest time, I Ignored my soul's quiet pleas for inner wellness. Becoming the quite literal manifestation of a weed within my own garden, due to neglecting the roots of

The Bec∞ming

my spiritual and authentic decline. The truth of my *why*, is within the shame of my experience, and the venomous belief that I have sown into myself that I am not worthy because of—blank. Blank has rested on a plate that I've served to myself as justification to avoid going backwards, despite it being for the sake of forward movement. I'm not sure how I *should* feel, now knowing that I have made a conscious decision to think myself into a reality that displeases me. I projected an image of who I thought I wanted to be, ignoring the true desires of my inner voice.

Through consistent practice I have become a master at identifying as a false representation of who Pashance is. Motivated and influenced by the caricature I've created that knows no shame, and should be loved by all, though unloved by self, in her truest form. It has taken years and countless attempts to articulate my story in a way that resonates with me and enriches my own understanding. Even so, I am sometimes still uncertain of how qualified I am to speak. Nonetheless, this is my attempt at obedience in spite of my discomfort. Gradually, I Am coming to understand that my duty is to do more than recite my story. To simply share is to bleed out, and onto another person. If I Am to be my own healer I must first:

- Identify the wound.
- Analyze the effects.
- Sterilize & bandage.

Pashance A.

- Implement a treatment plan.

In 2007, at just six years old, I was the eldest of my mother's two children. My brother Jullian, only a year younger, was not just my brother but my best friend. As a kid it seems so far-fetched for a direct, irreparable event to occur because this is the time when 'life is at its sweetest' so to speak. I can still see us, two carefree children running around the park in Linden projects, our laughter echoing as we chased each other until the street lights flickered on.

For blocks all you hear is "Avianna! Ceavian!" which officially calls our outdoor activity portion of the day to a close. We'd brush our teeth and ready ourselves for the next school day. Mom would read us stories as we lay in our bunk beds, and as soon as she'd leave, we would whisper to each other way past our bedtime until we finally fell asleep. Life was good. In our minds it would only get better; but then, it got worse first. On December 30th, 2007 Jullian fell sick again, a sadly frequent occurrence due to his condition. At birth Jullian was diagnosed with dextrocardia, so we frequented the doctors office. Obviously being so young, I didn't understand the severity of my baby brother's health issues. I only assumed that he had a stomach virus.

I remember going into our room that night before bed. On our boxed television I could see the DVD symbol over a blue screen. Jullian sat on the bottom bunk with a runny nose, wrapped up in his favorite red and blue blanket. His face was a bit darker than usual and his energy felt different. Considering he was always such a bright light in every room. It made me very anxious to see him that way, but all I could think of was the countless times I watched him exemplify courage and grace in moments where I thought he should be afraid, because *I was* afraid. I wanted him to feel strong, and loved because his strength, and his love was contagious to me. What I was feeling in that moment when I saw him, was probably nothing.

The last thing I said to Jullian before my mother sent me to bed in her room was "I love you, I will see you tomorrow". That night was the most stressful, uncomfortable, and scary of my little 6 years. I had no idea why I was so worried, until my parents got me out of bed on the rising of December 31st, to tell me that my little brother was in Heaven. This unimaginable loss shattered the very foundation of my home, deeply affecting my family and the entire community of Linden Projects. Every teacher, every student from our classes, family, friends and neighbors were all there for the passing of Jullian Ceavian Gamez. Our Forever 12~31 Angel.

After fourteen anniversaries I have begun to find ways to celebrate my brother's life and our relationship (with family, and on an individual basis), however, I still find myself in a cycle of good morning.

PASHANCE A.

NOTE: It is not my practice, but most people greet each other at the start of the day by saying *"good morning"*. In a literal sense, I began my day on December 31st in mourning. My opinion is likely to be controversial, but altering the spelling of a word doesn't change its core meaning—in this case to grieve.

Although I told my brother that I loved him before he passed away, I carry a lot of guilt with me anyway. Somehow, my little body knew that something was wrong, yet I stayed in bed despite this. I often rebuke myself for not being there with him when he took his last breath. For years I tortured myself with countless 'what if' scenarios about the nights leading up to New Years Eve, imagining how one different choice could have changed everything. If in any way I could have been a better big sister to him, and feeling like I failed as one because in my heart it was my job to protect my little brother, yet I wasn't there when he needed me most. I found myself damning the God I went to church to learn about every Sunday for taking him instead of me, when I was undoubtedly the less worthy child. My faith, already fragile, was destroyed first by my brother's death and then by my uncle's passing shortly after.

From here on, I began to isolate myself from my peers. I drilled into my mind that it was pointless to invest in anyone because *"they were just going to die anyway"*. Once I started changing residences, my new justification became *"I'm just going to move anyway"*. I

The Bec∞ming

never allowed myself to search for reasons to cultivate relationships because of how I imagined they'd turn out. My mind had become an empty playground, with no street lights, and no mom to call me back home.

This profound loss marked the beginning of my journey through grief and shaped my coping mechanisms in ways that I wouldn't fully understand until much later. Although my grades remained outstanding, and I was very active in school, I stayed in detention and ISS for the fights I'd get into. For me, staying in trouble was the only way that I felt seen because everyone was overcome by grief. I preferred to be disciplined than to feel ignored. I cried with a straight face, didn't speak one word, and did it all over again. As a woman today, these traumatic responses don't hold the same power over me, however they are still a hurdle for me to overcome. For example:

- In my present day, I still shy away from connections that require certain levels of trust and vulnerability. I love understanding other people's perspectives, and hearing of their passions; but I rarely go beyond that point.

- I Am more cognizant of how I respond to things that I don't like; however, I can be drawn to anger when my boundaries have been crossed, which is where my language still needs improvement.

- Sometimes I will feel emotionally heavy, yet refrain from expressing my feelings. I will oftentimes focus on a goal and offer my energy there, instead.

The next step, where I should sterilize and bandage my wound, is where I have found the greatest challenge because it requires a complete paradigm shift—starting at the root of the problem. The emptiness I felt the night my brother died was a wake-up call, pushing me toward a path of self-discovery and healing that would unfold in unexpected ways. This journey would lead to another pivotal moment—Operation Rehab.

The Bec∞ming

For the 6 year old Pashance,

Baby girl, you have merely scratched the surface of what is next to come. Please do not be afraid. There is still goodness in the world, and there is still goodness within you. I know that *'difficult'* is an understatement for what you have experienced. At this age, it's expected that your innocence and imagination will be the highlights of your life, however that not being *your* truth, doesn't mean that there's anything wrong with you. I need you to know that you are worthy of the love that you've convinced yourself is unattainable. You are right to acknowledge that people, places and circumstances are seasonal. Even temporary from the angle of life versus death; but I challenge that your perspective on the pointlessness of relationships is small minded. You are a little lady with great experience, but there is still much you do not know. The decision to allow yourself to love and be loved is a powerful one. You will later find that cultivating relationships will help you to overcome the dark times that you swear you're meant to endure alone. It is safe for you to experience others, and to allow them to experience you. Release those self-imposed limitations. Your future self will thank you.

You should know that everyone experiences anger, and in your case this type of response is expected. You've got all kinds of emotions running through you that you don't yet understand. If it is of any

PASHANCE A.

consolation, even when you're older and wiser, there may still be times where you scramble to interpret your own feelings. That is okay too. I need you to remind yourself that you are seen, you are heard, and you are understood. Even if it is by you, and God alone. Exercise your name because patience with yourself is most important. Impulsivity alongside idle hands are in fact the devil's workshop. Remember that before anyone else's voice is heard, yours is the first one that you hear, so be compassionate as well. This will create a safe space that allows the emotion which hides *behind* your anger to reveal itself properly. As you get older you will understand that emotional maturity is the willingness to experience every one of your emotions without judgment, and further improve upon how you respond to those feelings. Do not punish yourself for having them, or even for making mistakes. Take a pause. Breathe in. Make a better decision next time.

Lastly, my sweet girl, your feelings being a personal experience does not invalidate how real they are to you. Your voice, and that which rests within your heart, matter. Finding activities to pour your energy into can be healing, but be careful not to use them to overshadow the deeper issues that need your attention. You cannot place bandaids over shattered glass and expect it not to hurt when you drink. It is one thing to channel your energy into something, and another to seek distraction from it. I urge you to acknowledge the good, bad, and indifference of your thoughts and emotions. Allow yourself to experience them for a moment. Then set them free; and free you will be, in return.

Te Quiero…Mucho!

II

Operation Rehab

FACE ME SOBER

Pt. I

Today is a new day. I Am a new person; but, it's not quite what you think. The clock reads 4:16 PM as I slowly rise from a hospital bed. The sterile environment reflects the turmoil inside of me. This is not just a physical awakening, but a moment of profound self-realization because *"As a man thinketh, so is he"*. What have I been thinking? God introduces a simple concept to me, asking: *"Will I, or won't I accept this change today?"* I Am reminded that growth & comfort cannot dwell in the same space, and that although my transition *seems* intolerable, the decision to check my wounds or allow them to kill me, lives in the palms of my own hands. I ask myself, *"Am I willing to let my spirit die?"*

I Am learning that more than anything, my vessel is sensitive to energy. Especially, that of my own. The tenants residing within the walls of my mind, scribe tales of an all-powerful antagonist who gains purpose from the absence of heroes. This must be why my femininity refuses to bloom—this mental environment is not conducive to pure seeds. At this moment, I can hardly catch a breath. The landlord lines my tiles with gasoline and throws a book of lit matches down the stairs. A fire ignites in my heart as my throat cries for mercy at the rapid depletion of oxygen. I feel frantic. With each passing second, I grow more tired, eventually fading into oblivion.

As I reflect on those haunting 'what ifs', the scene shifts to April of 2016. I'm sitting in an empty room, lost in contemplation, questioning the choices that brought me here. The scent of rebellion lingers above my lips because the dangers of my secrets have yet to damage me beyond self-remedy. It has been two months since my mother contracted overseas, and somehow *I believe* that I Am equipped with sufficient knowledge from conversations I have never had. In my peripheral vision I see myself being primed. Just smart enough to vocalize a boundary, yet too weak to effectively enforce it, and so naive to believe that I'm still safe here. Unfortunately for me, I am temporarily immobilized. I cannot turn to save that silly girl. Unfortunately for her, my voice produces no sound.

PASHANCE A.

She cannot hear me shouting at her to run. Just as I always have, I stare in front of me with a blank face, no words, and gushing tears that swallow the ground beneath me. This time 2016, I am ignorant to the realms of sex and fondling, so what happens next was inconceivable to me. I remember having mentally replayed scenarios of attempted rapes and kidnappings growing up. In each scenario, I had a plan for my plan, but my ideas were always meant for the stranger who sought for me. I was never prepared for a wolf wearing sheep's cloth; however, I now know that he is most often the one to strip you of yourself, and then lure in the next sheep. Silly girl—this is NOT a game.

As I sit here in the void, forced to watch this play out, I become one with her again. Her arms are tired from fighting him off. The hand that shoves her head into the bed sheet is heavy as rocks. And once she realizes that she has lost—that this is happening, all I feel then, is her dead weight. Immediately after the breach, her soul joins me in oblivion for a few minutes of damning silence. When it is over she does not return immediately, so her vessel lay there frozen. The spirit looks to me as if to imply that *'what's understood doesn't need to be said'*, then proceeds to float away. I too begin regaining the function of my limbs, but I can feel her confusion—her rage—her hopelessness. As previously committed, my silly girl remains shackled to the detriment of her secrecy. Wanting to cry out for help, yet more afraid of humiliation—defamation. *"You know what, I'd rather attempt to clandestinely find the*

The Bec∞ming

answers to my queries because I don't want to admit that this happened to me. Can I pretend that nothing happened to me? I just want to forget". As I roll into the credits of this brutal memoir, I am yanked back from the void by the hands of an unsentimental doctor.

The aftermath of rape is an interesting thing to analyze. Whereas my spirit was able to dissociate from my body in the moment, I could never outrun the Pashance that I had become afterwards. For years, I found myself sizing up my own foot to fit into that person's shoes. Essentially, transforming into everything the perpetrator was, despite his absence. So, the bad guy lived on—through me.

I remember staying up for days on end from the constant nightmares. I lost my appetite almost entirely, and had no desire to do anything anymore. Not even the things that I once loved. My conversations with myself became extremely abusive, and that subsequently impacted my closest relationships as well. I hid beneath layers to avoid public attention, while I mutilated myself in private. I not only hated the experience. I hated myself for my ignorance. I hated him for violating me, and lying about it. I hated my mother for not preparing me, and moving me before I could take my finals. I hated my classmates for not defending my honor despite his admission of betrayal. I hated my teachers for their lack of empathy. I hated my step-dad for being distracted by the charm of the boy's mother. I hated the police officers

Pashance A.

assigned to my case because they did not believe me. I hated everything, pretty much.

Within this timeframe, doctors diagnosed me with PTSD and depression. It was in my *'best interest'* to see a therapist, yet somehow after speaking with her I still felt broken. All I could think of was how my virtue had been my greatest accomplishment in a school full of **real** fast girls & boys. I always thought I was better than my peers because I was the rare virgin. So evidently, and quite ironically, when my virtue was taken from me I had no clue who I was, or who I would be. My friend was my foe, but my killer was certainly my ignorance. I had no business being there; and the truth that I have been running from, is that I should have seen it coming. I just thought that my **No** was enough.

This was the first, almost fatal, blow to my ego.

My initial move from my first high school was to McDonough Georgia with my aunt and cousin. The love I received from them was patient, stern, supportive, and kind. Unfortunately, we lost touch when I had to move again, but I Am so grateful to have been loved by them at a time that I did not love myself. I pay homage to them both forevermore.

After McDonough, I found myself serving my sophomore year of high school in Stone Mountain. This residence was the complete opposite of that wholesome family living me and my little brother had come from. Draped in Christian cloth, was a family of more wolves. Their motive for vindictiveness, rooted in feuds before even my time. It seems as though the best way to hurt a woman is to attack her motherhood. What better way to achieve that than to lure her in with promise, so that she trusts you with her children? We endured verbal and psychological abuse unbeknownst to anyone beyond those damned doors. We were only allowed to shower a maximum of two-three times a week, for only 5 minutes at a time, and could only use a certain amount of squares of tissue in the restrooms. Given the secret war that these wolves had planned for my mother, they constantly punished me and my brother in ways tailored to destroy our sense of individualism. Until I could find a way to trap the wolf in his own deceptions, which I *eventually* did, we would continue to live in this hell hole.

In the midst of all of this, my education was of major concern. Due to missing my finals for the previous year, I had limited options for success, and a sour decision to make. I could either accept being held back, or take freshman & sophomore classes all at once for half the year. This was <u>in addition</u> to completing my prior finals. Suddenly, the one place that I felt I could go to escape my circumstances, had become yet another thing to stress about. Another thing to distract me from my healing. Albeit, I'd be damned to have been that smart and gotten left back for any reason, so I chose to face the challenge head on. On that day, however, I endured yet another blow to my ego.

Next came junior year, where I resided back in Brooklyn. It was nice to be back home, but I had honestly forgotten how much of a culture shock the education system was between states. Depending on your county, Georgia only required 26-32 credits to graduate. New York requires a minimum of 44 credits. My GPA had already dropped from a 4.0 to about a 2.8-3.0, and I only had 13 credits to my name. I can't blame my principal for speaking practically, but when I asked what I could do to expedite my graduation, his first response was *"it's not possible with these circumstances"* and suggested I settle for a potential mid-semester graduation for the next year. To be frank, I was so exhausted from fighting my way up in life, I just knew that I wouldn't last another year. I was willing to do whatever was necessary to leave high school early. Now on the contrary, school was also the only place that I was able to explore my talent and abilities, so the thought of a lack of direction afterwards raised an emotional response of its own.

I took honors, extra credit classes, added more subjects to my schedule, participated in clubs and in sports. I worked very hard my junior year. I often felt overwhelmed, but I kept pushing because I refused to be a super senior and I had a goal to achieve. Since I was a little girl I dreamed of graduating high school as Valedictorian, and from college as Summa Cum Laude. Realistically with my hand of cards, plus the many people who voiced their doubts of my achievement, I wasn't sure if I could accomplish part one. What I did know was that I was going to work like hell trying, and it paid off. By the third semester, I was a senior on the books.

The last few months of school I slipped back into depression; only showing up about two to three times a week. However, what most people didn't know was that behind closed doors, I was praying like nobody's business. By the strength of my God, I was completing the week's worth of assignments within the few days that I had shown face.

For the final weeks, I'd gotten some of that early year drive back because the time to name top classmen was approaching, and very intense. I held Valedictorian for the first few weeks, and you can only imagine how great I felt. However, although I got to experience that feeling for a moment, I concluded the year as 3rd of my class. This was still amazing considering all I'd gone through just to make it to the end, so I gladly celebrated that win. On June 26th 2018 by the grace of God and my efforts, I graduated with the seniors in my junior year of high school, and was privileged to give a graduation speech. By the end of the year, I had a 3.9 GPA, and drum roll please… a whopping 45 credits!

Pt. II

*M*y therapist used to tell me of the power that I had to reclaim my first sexual experience as the one that *I chose* to have. As expected it took me some years to make that decision, but the road to, and even afterward came with unfathomable challenges not aforementioned.

NOTE: Oftentimes people tend to label a response to an experience as **normal**, or **irregular**. I know this because I was once one of those people. What I have since learned is that it's easy to analyze what could've/would've/should've been done, when the situation in question is **Your Hypothetical,** and **Someone Else's Reality**. It is simply impossible to predetermine an individual's natural bodily response to **Fight**, **Flight**, or **Freeze** in a traumatic situation. In reality I froze, but in my hypothetical I was fighting. This is not a section to agree or disagree with. It just is. Please be empathetic if you proceed.

Although I abstained from sexual activity for a long time, my body was very confused. The hormonal changes I underwent absolutely disgusted me because I expected my body to be as discerning as my mind, by responding to the trauma only. That wasn't quite the case, and frankly, it just provided more ammunition for my self-hatred. In my eyes I was damaged goods unable to be restored. So, the next step for me was to escape that feeling. I had tried once before, but soon realized that I was too afraid to end my own life. My improvisation was finding ways to *tolerate* my existence, which for me looked like high-grade, black & milds, and alcohol. My mother often affirmed that my pain was intended to be a catalyst for my growth, but for a long time I wasn't ready to receive that. It made me feel like I wasn't being listened to. Are you listening to me, Avianna?

{If you are struggling with thoughts of self harm, please talk to someone! You deserve to live. Just hold on! I promise all will be well, and much sooner than you think! You Are Loved.}

Progressing down the timeline (post-consent) I must say, experience only revealed more symptoms! I notice that the longer I refuse to address the root of the issue, it simply finds other ways to grab my attention. So, let's backtrack a bit.

My first signal was indubitably my hypersexuality. I glorified the perverted identity of sex, which is lust, and disguised it as *'sacred union'* to trick my psych into allowing me to proceed. I realized that sex had simply become a more matured version of escapism for me. I was intoxicated by the instant gratification of fucking because it was a pleasurable distraction, and I too was intoxicating when it came time to deliver.

Pashance A.

I ponder whether subconsciously I've been trying to replace my memory of rape, with the vision that I have for my love life through a misprescribed lens. The problem with that is, I can't force a circle into a square, and I can't move onto the next grade if I don't pass my core classes. A lesson not learned, is forever a lesson repeated. Transparently, maybe obviously, I've been more afraid of surrendering than the pain that I've caused myself in my defiance.

Considering the coping mechanisms that I chose, I wonder if the reason I've felt that no-one truly listened to me, was because I never actually listened to myself. It is an interesting notion though because despite the fact that I've neglected myself emotionally, I have still accomplished many of my goals. Therefore I pose the question of whether it's possible that my mind now associates neglect with opportunity, due to my casual transition into aspired results. These experiences have challenged me in many ways. Some that I am still reluctant to share, however a few relevant examples include:

- I generally avoid bold colors or styles because I don't want to draw the attention of those who will sexualize, and potentially cause me harm. I often immediately recognize men as a threat, and consequently shield myself instead of allowing myself the freedom to embody full confidence in my boldness.

The Bec∞ming

- In some situations where I had no desire to have sex, I allowed it to happen anyway. I didn't believe in the power of my own tongue to authoritatively say no, nor in the discipline of the man to respect it. I figured it would be more traumatic if I said no and was overpowered, than if I just let it happen.

- At times my inner voice is still a reflection of how I felt *while* being raped. Helpless, weak, incapable. And not because these things are true, but because when I found the courage to ask for help I was told that I *"probably wanted it, and changed my mind at the last second"*. Because almost all the adults that I cried to, called or viewed me as a liar; and because I didn't have enough physical strength to maintain my fight against him. This abusive language has traveled a distance with me, but I now make efforts to affirm myself otherwise.

- I used to be terrified of sleeping because of the nightmares that awaited me. I still have those nightmares, but now as an adult I endure them to sleep away my pain.

- I do not trust anyone to take care of my heart as I do. Consequently, I condition myself for an isolated life, although my desire is to connect with others of like-hearted nature.

Pashance A.

For the 14 year old Pashance,

Well baby girl... you're a woman now. I know that this happened in the worst way, but now it's time for us to have some woman to woman conversation. So, put your seatbelt on.

Prior to this pivotal stage in your life, you were a passenger riding down a highway that you had never seen before. Now, you are the driver, and this comes with a huge responsibility. When you become one with your vehicle, you are responsible for the safety of everyone within it, to include other drivers on the road. You will quickly learn that you'll never be able to control how other people drive; however, you *can* hone your skills to create the best experience for all. Cognizance will keep you safe, and the signs around will guide you to your destination. All you must do is pay attention. Then make the next best, and informed decision.

I use this analogy because it gently introduces the concept of **accountability**. Your vehicle represents Your Temple. The Highway represents a world of New Experiences. The Other Drivers represent External Circumstances that are Beyond Your Control. Your graduation from passenger to Driver represents that which is now *Within* Your Control. The Signs represent Your Intuition, and Cognizance is the Awareness Of Your Surroundings, equipping you with the tools necessary to make good decisions.

The Bec∞ming

> I hear you, Avianna. I Am listening, and I Am with you. Now it is your turn to listen.

Your intuition is one of your greatest superpowers because it is a direct channel to the Divine Consciousness. Sometimes your intuition speaks, while on other occasions she is a nagging feeling inside of you. However she shows up, I can assure you that your best decisions are a result of listening to her. The equal opposite is that your greatest regrets will be a consequence of self negligence, such as this one. You must **always** use discernment. Do not ever place yourself in an environment where your safety can be compromised. Remember that what happened to you is not your fault, nor does it define who you are.

Affirm: I Am Strong. I Am Brave. I Am Rising Like a Phoenix.

These affirmations will carry you through life's upcoming challenges.

You will realize sooner than you think, that life does not stop simply because you're hurting. Things are going to get harder before they get easier, and it is going to *feel* unfair. Nonetheless, I assure you that when the time comes for you to face the next thing, you will be ready. Now, despite what you may be thinking, I'm not referring to external factors as I foreshadow these challenges. I Am referring to the war within. See, God has a system. No matter how far you run, or for how long you run, the things that you avoid will always catch up with you. The only way to escape the maze is to practice forgiveness. Trust me, I know how crazy and vague that sounds, so let's get into it.

Each time you've had a negative experience, it chipped away at your innocence and changed how you view the world around you. Potentially even how you view yourself. Your lens now only sees monsters and danger, and this perspective strips you of the life that you deserve. I want you to try using a different lens. Bear with me now. It's easy to view people as monsters when they hurt you because it justifies the anger and resentment that you choose to hold on to. Before you argue me down, it is indeed a choice because even when that person is long gone, you still live as if they're present. The most challenging, yet necessary parts of healing, are to:

Humanize the people that cause you the most harm.

AND

Remind yourself that the trauma is a Memory. Not a present circumstance.

To address the first matter: we all have reasons as to why what we've done makes sense to us, as well as a tailor-made compass of good and evil. Suppose these monsters whom you carry hatred for, are actually just human beings making stupid mistakes. Although these mistakes hurt, and may even be traumatic, can you hold compassion for another human being? Lest you become a monster by circumstance, for the person whom you considered to be a monster by nature.

For the second matter: when you operate in your present day as if the trauma remains, you imprison yourself on each dimensional plane. This means that your mind has become a weapon, and its target is your own body. This subsequently instigates physical illness, and stunts your emotional and spiritual ascension. In even simpler terms, the enemy that was once outside of you, is now within you, which causes more damage. In conclusion, how distinguishable could you possibly be from them, if you allow yourself to become what you loathe? Please inner-stand that I speak to you from a place of love, and that this mental shift does not justify behavioral misconduct. This is a pathway to healing *your* Mind, Body, and Spirit which in due time, will cause the transformation of your personal reality. *You* get to choose whether to repeat a cycle, or to find another way. There is always another way.

Lastly, you must know that no-one is coming to save you, my love. It is a harsh reality, but you *must* save yourself. You are not a victim. You are an overcomer—a conqueror. So with this in mind, are you going to roll over and give up, or choose to see the stars as you take your power back? Your freedom awaits your relentless pursuit. The bargain with God is to humbly surrender to what is calling you, so that

Pashance A.

you may receive what is waiting for you on the other side of your pain. You can do this, Avianna. I believe in you.

III

Uprooting This House

MIRROR MY MIRROR

Lately, I've been in conflict with myself regarding the concept of "standards". My standards, even. Although they're necessary to the degree of moral compass, these standards have been the very reason for some of my more recent dissatisfactions. I hope to make good decisions, however I am currently unsure of what that looks like. Am I foolish to walk away from a person or situation that I Am content with, due to a desire for something more? Am I operating from my ego and self-sabotaging, or have I claimed dominion over my life, by seeking to create a reality that I find most fulfilling? There is a very thin line here, and I Am contemplating what I "should" do, versus what my heart actually wants.

The Bec∞ming

I have adopted an unrealistic, superficial love compass. Although substance was always a subconscious desire of mine, my conscious pursuits mirrored something different. I constantly found myself in unrequited situations, and due to my cognitive dissonance I hadn't realized that each of those experiences were a reflection of unresolved matters within me. I've borne the insecurities of my past like luggage into my present day, chasing the stupefaction from a fantasy where I've acquired my wants, whilst simultaneously blind to the neglect of my needs. I've never allowed myself to acknowledge Pashance, nor any other person for who they truly are, but rather, for how our separate histories and deluded character representatives could align. It became second nature to make my personal desires optional, due to my misconception regarding what partnership "should" look like in order to breed success in love. The reality of this practice was simply me transforming the gravitational pull of two traumatic stories, into one traumatic bond. In this way, I've become the bearer of my own disappointments.

I now pose the question to myself of whether the unresolved matter within me is abandonment trauma. My Mind and Spirit have been out of alignment because I had convinced myself that I was not deserving of the desires of my soul. As I grew accustomed to abandonment during maturation, it further distorted my perception of love. I began to radiate and attract mirroring energy because I had given the trauma the power to rewrite the vision of my future, based upon that which it sought to change about my past. I denied myself a full experience of self-love due to the unfortunate belief that my Moon energy was not as beautiful as my Sun. I realize now, in this uprooting, that it is time to address my scarcity mindset. To heal my fears surrounding loss, and redefine what it actually means to lose.

I have remained in situations with people, places and things far beyond the date of expiry, in efforts to avoid the grief that I knew was on its way. Yet, if I had simply allowed my intuition to guide me opposite of unworthy investments, grief would not even be part of the equation. What I'm beginning to find most interesting as I dig through this dirt, is how my decisions and lack thereof created an inner environment where the subtlety of my own spiritual voice, fell upon deaf ears. Oftentimes I would wait for a scream, then find myself trying to outrun accountability, knowing that the whispers should have been enough to capture my attention.

I Am learning now that I can't force anyone to fit the vision that I've created for my own life, and vice versa. That I can only choose *if,* and *how,* to proceed with them. Despite its simplicity, this construct has actually been quite challenging for me. Instead of allowing my experiences to unfold naturally, I attempted to assort people and things into the areas of my life that I wanted them to serve in because my ego felt safe with what I could control. This practice led to

Divine intervention many times, and would continue until I gained self-awareness.

When I first became privy to this pattern of mine, I thought that the necessary changes I should make required coupled resolutions and common grounds. So initially, I did a lot of talking, not realizing that all the resolution that I needed was within me alone. I Am the only person in the world that can hear my intuition, and I take it that God designed things that way for a reason. It is when I stray from my own mind that I stand for nothing, and fall for everything. I must practice stillness. Otherwise, how much longer will I express the willingness to compromise my own values for the sake of crippling attachments? Why have I chosen to trade my self-worth for the currency of someone else's affections, and how did my misrepresentation of Love get so far gone? It is safe to say that the foundation I have built thus far, is not stable.

I've noticed within myself, and in others, that relationships are often pursued for validation rather than companionship. Thus, most people enter the union broken. I do believe that it's still possible to create something from that brokenness, however I Am learning that the success of any ship (whether it be professional, platonic, romantic or familial) is contingent upon each individual's success at being single. In our singleness we find the opportunity to build our first relationship, which is the one that we have with the God who dwells within thyself. On **The Journey to Bec∞ming** we master the self, and

Pashance A.

ultimately release what is meant to be healed by God's hands, and not our own, with love and grace. I do not dishonor myself for not being what others desire of me. Rather, I becoome myself by honoring what is true to me. What I master in my independence reflects positively in my union, whereas if I am building from my brokenness I will always look to my person to fix me, or vice versa. As adults we get to choose whether or not to create our own inner stability. However, that which we practice in our adulthood is often a reflection of what we've learned as children. There is less collateral damage, even *'seasoned codependency'*, when the home foundation is built and nurtured on stable grounds. That being said, where the hell are the heads of these houses?

The achievement of my soul's desires is fully contingent upon my willingness to apply the wisdom that I've garnered. I Am willing, now. I understand that my **Knowledge** creates a sturdy foundation. My **Understanding** of that knowledge fills me. With **Wisdom** I create equilibrium, and align with the desires of my soul. I Am, in fact, deserving of the love that I envision myself having, without the settlement. That is, the love I honor myself with, and that which I accept from others. A pint sized portion is incapable of filling a gallon sized container, so I Am wise to consider both the substantiality, and sustainability of something that is rooted from incompatible visions.

IV

Bloom

LIKE A LOTUS

God has been telling me to check for weeds in my garden. That I need to be alone for a while. I must admit though, I have been resistant.

The conversation between my mind and soul has been incredibly disputatious. Impeding on my ability to make sound decisions. My mind presents me with several doubts, while my soul urges me to have faith and trust in my process. It's a bit strange how within me there seems to be two polar opposite energies. The one who doubts and does most of the speaking, and the one who has a knowing while simply observing said speech. *"Pride cometh before a fall"* the Lord says to me. There's a difference between being alone, and being lonely. I find that they only feel the same when I don't like the person I am alone with. This *must* still be applicable when I am the only party involved, and it reflects my true esteem. I Am learning that the voice of God is most clear when I Am quiet. Still, and without distraction. When truly grounded, there will be no influence powerful enough to overshadow the essence of God that dwelleth in me. So until then, this is my season to master my silence. My year in white.

Naturally, my doubts stem from my demographic background and the memory of my life experiences. However, the scripture that says that *"faith is the substance of things hoped for, and the evidence of things not seen",* challenges my insecurities. It seems that I've disconnected from the part of myself that produces hope from my imaginative state, as a result of outsourcing for a knowing that is already inside. I Am energy, and energy is weightless. It lives in, yet is not of this world, so it cannot be measured, created or destroyed. Understanding who I Am at the core of my existence, transforms my physical and metaphysical ability to give and receive, through my connection with all things from God-source. I have learned that my offerings to the universe can either come from a place of lack or a place of abundance. Meaning that if I lack self-love, I will wander aimlessly, as I have been, fully misguided and in search of a harvest that I will fail to recognize upon reaching it. Contrarily, if I love myself abundantly, I need only prepare myself to receive because the harvest will always search for, and find me. The evidence of things not seen, is the

Pashance A.

provision of my will to dream, as God strips down my fleshly inhibitions.

I have questioned my worthiness more often than I'm proud of, asking things like:

"Why Am I not enough", "What Am I missing?", "Who Am I, really?"

I Am still gaining an understanding of Agape Love. I Am grateful to now know what it is not because that process *equally* brings me closer to the God within. Although part of me feels ashamed by the admission of my self-doubt, there is also another part of me that feels free. A subtle beauty lives in the queries of my shadow-self because now I Am certain about where my answers come from. I understand that my experiences with others are a mirror of how I love myself, and that while love has its challenges, it is not meant to be hard. Now more than ever, I understand that some things about the world will not change until we all learn to harmonize our Divine trinity. With that in mind, *I* Am fully capable of changing the way that *I* think, the way that *I* see, and the way that *I* respond. There is a saying that *"femininity blooms in the right environment"*, yet in the most unseemingly of such is when my light shines brightest. The darkness that I thought would consume me, and prevent my light from shining, created the exact conditions necessary to make me bloom. And bloom, I will.

V

Good Morning

THE UNFINISHED WORK

In this chapter of my life, I Am learning to see beyond my lens of survival. This mindset has protected me for a long time, however there have also been instances where operating in survival mode has hindered me. My responsibility now is to clearly identify and determine <u>when</u> and <u>where</u> there is a need. I want to know what it is to *live* my life, not just exist and survive.

I have practiced ignoring the voice of my past self. My *'inner child'*, if you will. As a result, my body is making adjustments to protect me from malfunction, synonymously, the danger that I continuously project through my own subconscious mind. My physical experience is safe for my indulgence, however I am challenged by my prior conditioning. I've been throwing swords and knuckles in the fight to survive, though today that war is but a memory. How do I realign my mind, body, and spirit with the present moment? How do I calm my defensive reflexes and reassure my temple that all is well? It's time I reevaluate my priorities.

I received a word from God recently with a suggestion that I *"embrace new levels of vulnerability; and that I set, and honor healthier boundaries in my life."* My interpretation of this wisdom was initially flawed because I made it applicable to matters outside of me, though the assignment truly spoke of inner work. Disregarding the need for my "inner child" to be heard reflected a refusal of vulnerability with even myself. I hear the Lord saying: *"How can I love what you are afraid of showing me?"* Now drawn to the story of Adam and Eve, and their nakedness before God prior to eating the forbidden fruit, I Am intrigued by the implication that God was trying to protect the innocence of mankind. Man decided that our nakedness should be covered from the sight of God, although that which we try to hide are exactly the things loved most. The imperfection *in* the perfect work is what the creator finds most endearing. I see now, that vulnerability is the only ingredient that God requires in order to prepare the recipe for miracles. I personally used to believe vulnerability to be weakness, but in actuality, it is a form of bravery that leads to freedom, and softens the heart enough for God to enter. The act of relinquishing a shield (which is the urge to preserve oneself), and face that which could possibly inflict wounds while seemingly unprotected, is faith in its truest respect.

Furthermore, boundaries are equally an internal assignment because every human being was gifted with free will. When entering a new season in my life, I must first ask: *"Am I holding myself accountable to my personal boundaries?"* Then, I must determine whether or not the person I am engaging with equally respects those boundaries. Finally, I must surrender to the reality of what is, and make the next best decision for me. I Am learning to allow the experiences that find me (whether good, bad, or indifferent), and to release my expectations with a willingness to start over and do it all again. All without dwelling on the infinite probable realities that do not belong to me. For the most part, I have been willing to start over. Though mainly under very specific conditions, which fully counteracts Agape Love. That being the case, how have I expected to reap a love that I have not sown into The Universe? My healthy exchanges of transparency welcome life, love, and an opportunity to experience the beauty amidst the world's chaos. Moreover, others learn how to treat me based upon the healthy boundaries that I personally uphold. Too much, or too little of either of these things, has the potential to knock me off my axis, so let's get grounded.

First things first, we've all heard the saying that *'words are spells'*, but that terminology tends to have some extremely negative connotations. I would like to introduce the perspective that words are plants. That they are living, breathing beings. This is important because a plant grows from a seed, obviously, but irrespective of controversy, seeds are not bound by limitations. Meaning, that a seed can be planted both physically, and metaphysically through thought and speech. If I am not careful about the seeds that I plant in my mind, or those that I allow to be planted into my ear by others, these seeds will become an infection for my thoughts. That seed will then travel from my mind into my heart, where it will take root and develop into an intimate feeling. *"Out of the abundance of the heart the mouth speaks"*, so that infected seed that I have spoken has manifested into a living, breathing thing that is now attached to my journey. This wisdom took a while to make a connection with me, but I Am now here. The appointed time for it to resonate with my spirit.

Despite my fleshly reservations regarding my next steps, I know and understand the patterns that must change. I must be intentional about what I feed my mind daily, and practice living in flow with The Universe. Rejection is Divine protection, and all that is meant to be will find me. So, in fact, all things work together for my highest good, and the highest good of all. I Am learning that the freedom to live is something that only I can give to myself. I used to place that responsibility and my fears onto a misguided perception of God-source as an external energy, then blame my outcomes on that believed external force that *'only occasionally'* had my best interest. However

Pashance A.

the truth is, that Celestial energy dwells within me, and all other things connected to the creator. God is not an external force of nature, which means that the blame, fear, and responsibility that I attempted to give away, all belong to me. It is why *my* decisions create the reality that *I* experience. The power of God and the encounter with Heaven are both inner happenings, so my fear was not that *"the Lord would let me down"*, but really that I would let myself down. My ego just needed someone else to blame.

I have endured some hard hitters to my ego throughout my life. Yet, wounded and tired, she still stands. I have finally figured out that *I* must be the one to put her to rest. Otherwise, she will continue fighting, as she was designed to do. I realize that I've allowed people and things to take their shots at her because I believed that to kill my ego it had to hurt. The truth is that it doesn't. My ego is simply the survivor in me, the warrior sworn to protect my heart until I decide to relieve her. She dies only at the hands of love, and grace. My Love, and My Grace. I must only be courageous enough to see her, acknowledge where she comes from and why she remains. The reality is that the more my ego wins, the greater the expense of my spiritual development. So, I Am eulogizing the version of Pashance that I once had to be. I thank you for loving me, and walking this journey patiently and diligently with me. I release you, and simultaneously embrace the new version of Pashance that awaits my becoming. Between fear and forward motion, familiarity and the unknown, I Am choosing the latter for both. Only new. Only better.

VI

Baptized In Light

TRANSFORMATION BUTTERFLY

I have taken the last few months to focus on recentering my energies. This process has been occasionally overwhelming, yet predominantly enlightening and beautiful. I have made plenty of mistakes within this time frame, and I have learned from them. As of now, I Am free of my once desperate need for controlled substances. **My Mind Is Clear and Strong**. I now allow myself to enjoy more of what I love, and I am gradually exploring increased physical activity. It is normal for me to begin my day with a smudge stick, a hot cup of natural tea, and a barefoot walk through the grass as I visualize my intentions for the day ahead. **My Body Is In Perfect Health, and A Magnet For Abundance**. When I experience fear, sadness, or anger, I channel that energy into the Divine natures of strength, joy, passion and hope. I embrace my emotions for the fullness of what they are, and the fullness of what they can be. **My Emotions Are My Link To Co-Creation With God-source.** I apply Stillness into my daily life for the activation and clarity of Ajna and Sahasrara within my soul. **My Spirit Is Whole, and One With The Divine Consciousness.**

I Am beginning to know and understand Divine Feminine energy personally. She is a gift. The purest expression of my identity. Concurrently, I Am learning to honor my Divine Masculine energy without it superseding my femininity. Admittedly, it is challenging at times, considering my background and the neural rewiring I Am undergoing; however, my focus today is on my process, rather than the results that I can only hope for with no way of actually seeing. I Am more gentle and patient with myself today. I understand that throughout this journey there will be plenty of things that require my attention, dedication and even resilience. Also that I need only to take each day in stride, with certainty that I Am exactly when and where I'm supposed to be. I know now that the concept of time is simply a third dimensional construct that was formulated for ordinary human understanding. This influences my belief as to why scripture suggests *"lean not unto thine own."* God does not wear a watch because time is fluid. My prior misconception was that my intuition leads to a point in time, when really, the intuitive state leads me towards purpose; according to the path(s) that I choose to take of course.

Given the many hardships of my personal life experience, I have often been told to "change my narrative". Transparently speaking, I didn't understand what that meant until recently. In 2020, I made my first attempt at "changing my narrative" with a book that I wrote called "I Am Healed. Encouraged. Risen." At that time I was still locating my voice, so I lived vicariously through the characters that I had created. It was at the beginning of my **Journey to Becoming** where I thought that "changing my narrative" was an opportunity to give someone else the truth of a circumstance that I didn't want, and be healed by the triumph that I wrote for them, yet was unable to give to myself. The truth is that I couldn't get full from simply watching someone else eat. I had to do the work, and it wasn't until my acceptance of this that I began to ask the right questions.

"If this isn't it, what do I think it looks like?"

"What does it feel like, maybe?"

"As a matter of fact, what does it sound like to change my narrative?"

Interestingly, engaging all of my senses for this intangible concept is what guided me properly over time.

The Bec∞ming

Now quite ironically, after the most difficult experiences of my past, The Universe had a strange way of always placing me in close proximity to the environment with which the trauma had taken place. I believe that this was God's way of testing the authenticity of my progress because I quickly learned that it is easy to claim being healed when I Am no longer required to physically face old wounds. For as long as I can remember, my only stories were of pain and grief, but today, I dare to embrace new ones. To write and share a story that *I* find worthy of telling. One of true self-love. The wisdom that I Am unveiling is that we are hardly ever *fully* ready for the next step because there are so many unspoken facets of healing. The key for me was when I became ready enough, and was able to summon just a little bit of courage, I did it despite my fear.

I have come to terms with the beautiful fact that I Am a woman now. I may no longer, nor do I have any desire, to run away from myself, or freeze up when it's time for me to make decisions and be held accountable for my choices. The fight that I have in me now, is a spiritual one. I Am honest with myself about my growth and the lack thereof. I acknowledge all of my thoughts, feelings and behaviors, and work every day to align them with The Divine. I know now, and understand what it means to change my narrative: It is to release all that the past has told me that I would become. To make an unyielding, new, and better decision to achieve the desires of my soul

Pashance A.

as a light-worker. I no longer wonder what my life could have been had things gone differently. Instead, I ponder what my life *will* be, now that I Am free, finally. *I* define who Pashance Avianna is. Not my past, and not people's perceptions of who I "should" be. Although there is still a lot for me to learn, and much longer a journey to walk, I trust wholeheartedly that I Am ready to welcome the fulfillment that God has in store for me. For the first time, **I Am. I Do. I Feel. I Love. I Speak. I See. I Understand Inner Peace.**

The Bec∞ming

My intention for those who embark on this **Journey to Bec∞ming** with me, is to cultivate a community of people who embody Agape Love. When we learn to and assiduously practice healing the trinity of our own Mind Body and Spirit, we metaphysically shift the atmosphere responsible for changing the physical experience. My reality is a byproduct of the energy that I emit into the Divine Universal Consciousness. As does this fact apply to all human beings, given the dominion we've been granted among other forms of life. Metamorphosis Diaries as a whole, is the documented journey of my spiritual ascension over time, as I conduct my shadow work in real time.

Although the foundation, and explorations of my spirituality may differ from others, I believe that we are all connected. That we are not defined by where we come from or our experiences, but rather by who and how we love, and what we choose to be. I hope to leave you inspired to love yourself and others, as God so loves the world. Equally knowing that your process is beautiful no matter how chaotic, or different from others it may be. Understand that the **Journey to Bec∞ming** is not a straight shot upward. There are and always will be a few dips along the way. Nonetheless, I know that you and I both are ready for all that awaits. If only you could see how perfect your imperfections actually are. Trust that all things work together for good.

Love,

Pashance A.

To Be Continued…

The Becooming

Pashance A.

Pashance A.

Metamorphosis Diaries

Book I

Made in the USA
Columbia, SC
12 August 2024